OXFORD VOCAL MUSIC

LIBBY LARSEN

Try Me, Good King

Last Words of the Wives of Henry VIII

For Solo Soprano and Piano

D1568109

OXFORD
UNIVERSITY PRESS

Try Me, Good King

LIBBY LARSEN

Premiered by Meagan Miller, soprano, and Brian Zeger, piano, at the Juilliard Theatre on 19 January 2001 for the Marilyn Horne Foundation's Eighth Annual New York Recital

Program Note

Divorce, behead, die, divorce, behead, die. This grade-school memory game is how I first came to know about the six wives of Henry VIII, King of England from 1509–1547. Since then, I've been fascinated with the personal consequences of power that befell the Tudor family and the circle of political intrigue of both church and state, which caused such turmoil in the private lives of Henry and his queens.

Try Me, Good King is a group of five songs drawn from the final letter and gallows speeches of Katherine Aragon, Anne Boleyn, Jane Seymour, Anne of Cleves, and Katherine Howard. Henry's sixth wife, Katherine Parr, outlived him and brought some domestic and spiritual peace into Henry's immediate family. Although her written devotions are numerous, her role in the story of the Henry's wives is that of a peaceful catalyst. In these songs I chose to focus on the intimate crises of the heart that affected Henry's first five wives. In a sense, this group of songs is a monodrama of anguish and power.

I've interwoven a lute song into each song, including John Dowland's "In darkness let me dwell" (Katherine of Aragon and Katherine Howard), Dowland's "If my complaints" (Anne Boleyn), Michael Praetorius's "Lo, how a Rose e'er blooming" (Jane Seymour), and Thomas Campion's "I care not for these ladies" (Anne of Cleves). These songs were composed during the reign of Elizabeth I, and while they are cast as some of the finest examples of the golden age, they also create a tapestry of unsung words, which comment on the real situation of each doomed queen.

Two other musical gestures unify the songs: first, the repeated note recalls the lute and creates psychological tension; second, an abstract bell-tolling punctuates each song and releases the spiritual meaning of the words.

It is an honor to create new work for Meagan Miller and Brian Zeger and contribute to the ongoing vision of the Marilyn Horne Foundation.

— Libby Larsen

TRY ME, GOOD KING
Last Words of the Wives of Henry VIII
For Solo Soprano and Piano

Katherine of Aragon

Katherine of Aragon to Henry VIII,
7 January 1536

Libby Larsen

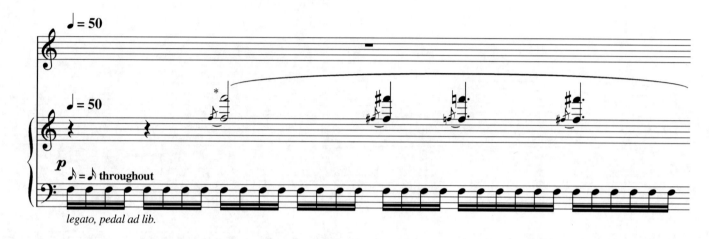

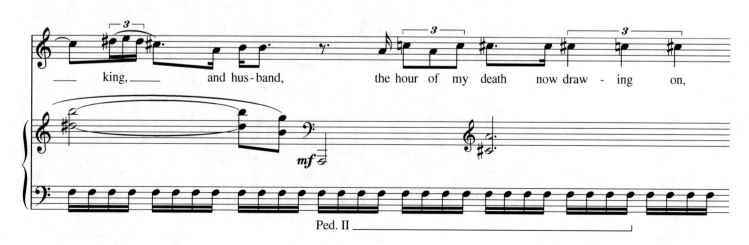

*"In darkness let me dwell," John Dowland

Printed in the U.S.A.

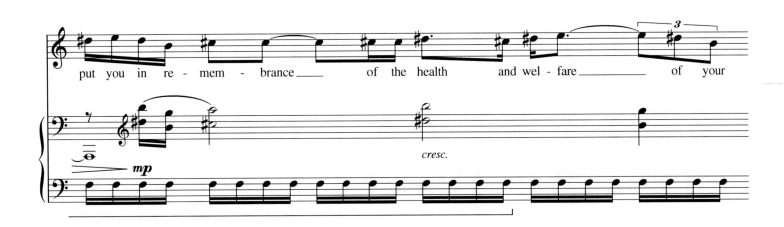

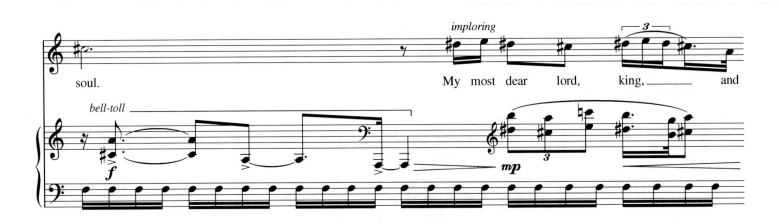

*"In darkness let me dwell"

*"In darkness let me dwell"

Anne Boleyn

Anne Boleyn to Henry VIII, 6 May 1536;
Henry's love letter to Anne Boleyn;
Anne Boleyn execution speech, 19 May 1536

Libby Larsen

*"If my complaints," John Dowland

Jane Seymour

Jane Seymour to the Council,
  12 October 1537;
"Tudor Rose," Anonymous

Libby Larsen

Right, trust - y   and Well Be-lov - ed, __   we greet you well, ____

for   as   much   as   be the in - es-ti-ma-ble good-ness   of   Al - might-y God, ____

*"Lo, how a Rose e're blooming," Michael Praetorius

push ahead

Joyed may we be, our ___ prince ___ to see, and ___

ros - - - - - - es

three. ___

(Hum) ___

push ahead

bell-toll

bell-toll

rit.

rit.

bell-toll

a tempo

gently

a tempo

p

rit.

rit.

bell-toll

p

very gently

Anne of Cleves

Anne of Cleves to Henry VIII,
11 July 1540

Libby Larsen

*"I care not for these ladies," Thomas Campion

20

Katherine Howard

Recorded at her execution
by an unknown Spaniard,
13 February 1541

Libby Larsen

*"In darkness let me dwell," John Dowland

long be-fore the King_ took me, I loved_ Tho-mas Cul-pep-er.

I wish to God I had done as Cul-pep-er wished me,

for at the time the King_ want-ed me, Cul-pep-er urged me to

say that I was pledged to him._

26

*"In darkness let me dwell"

Libretto

Katherine of Aragon (1485–1536)
Queen from June 1509 to January 1533

Katherine of Aragon, formerly Queen of England, to King Henry VIII, 7 January 1536

My most dear Lord, King, and Husband,

The hour of my death now drawing on, the tender love I owe you forces me . . .
to commend myself unto you and to put you in remembrance of the health and
welfare of your soul. . . . You have cast me into many calamities and yourself into
many troubles. For my part, I pardon you everything, and I wish to devoutly pray
God that He will pardon you also. For the rest, I commend unto you our daughter,
Mary, beseeching you to be a good father unto her. . . . Lastly, I make this vow, that
my eyes desire you above all things. . . .

Anne Boleyn (1502?–1536)
Queen from January 1533 to May 1536

Letter from Anne Boleyn, Queen of England, to Henry VIII, 6 May 1536;
Excerpts from two letters from Henry VIII to Anne Boleyn;
Anne Boleyn's speech at her execution, 19 May 1536

Try me, good king, . . . and let me have a lawful trial, and let not my . . . enemies
sit as my accusers and judges. . . . Let me receive an open trial for my truth shall
fear no open shame. . . . Never a prince had a wife more loyal in all duty, . . . in all
true affection, than you have ever found in Anne Bulen . . . . You have chosen me
from low estate to be your wife and companion. . . . Do you not remember the
words of your own hand? "My own darling . . . I would you were in my arms . . .
for I think it long since I kissed you. My mistress and friend. . . ." Try me, good
king. . . . If ever I have found favor in your sight—if ever the name of Anne Bulen
has been pleasing to your ears—then let me obtain this request. . . and my
innocence shall be . . . known and . . . cleared.

Good Christian People, I come hither to die, . . . and by the law I am judged
to die. . . . I pray God save the King. I hear the executioner's good, and my neck
is so little. . . .

Jane Seymour (c.1506–1537)
Queen from May 1536 to October 1537

Jane Seymour, Queen of England, to the Council, 12 October 1537;
"Tudor rose" (Anonymous)

Right trusty and Well-Beloved, we greet you well . . . for as much as be the ines-
timable goodness . . . of Almighty God, we be delivered . . . of a prince, . . .

I love the rose both red and white.
To hear of them is my delight!
Joyed may we be,
Our prince to see,
And roses three!

Anne of Cleves (1515–1557)
Queen from January 1540 to July 1540

Anne of Cleves, Queen of England, to Henry VIII, 11 July 1540

I have been informed . . . by certain lords . . . . of the doubts and questions which
have been . . . found in our marriage . . . . It may please your majesty to know that,
though this case . . . be most hard . . . and sorrowful . . . I have and do accept
[the clergy] for my judges. So now, . . . the clergy hath . . . given their sentence,
I . . . approve . . . . I neither can nor will repute myself for your grace's wife . . .
yet it will please your highness to take me for your sister, for which I most humbly
thank you. . . .

Your majesty's most humble sister,
Anne, daughter of Cleaves

Katherine Howard (1521–1542)
Queen from July 1540 to February 1541

Recorded at her execution by an unknown Spaniard, 13 February 1541

God have mercy on my soul. Good people, I beg you pray for me. By the journey
upon which I am bound, brothers, I have not wronged the King. But it is true that
long before the King took me, I loved [Thomas] Culpeper. . . . I wish to God I had
done as Culpeper wished me, for at the time the King wanted . . . me, [Culpeper]
urged me to say that I was pledged to him. If I had done as he wished me I should
not die this death, nor would he. . . . God have mercy on my soul. Good people, I
beg you pray for me. . . . I die a Queen, but I would rather die the wife of Culpeper.